Eleanor Roosevelt

Introduction

Eleanor Roosevelt was the niece of one U.S. president, Theodore Roosevelt, and married a man who would become another, Franklin D. Roosevelt.

Redefining the role of the first lady, she advocated for human and women's rights, held press conferences and penned her own column.

After leaving the White House in 1945, Eleanor became chair of the U.N.'s Human Rights Commission. The groundbreaking first lady died in 1962 in New York City.

"Have convictions. Be friendly. Stick to your beliefs as they stick to theirs. Work as hard as they do."— Eleanor Roosevelt

This is the descriptive, concise biography of Eleanor Roosevelt.

Table of Contents

Introduction 1
Table of Contents.. 2
Eleanor Roosevelt 3
Personal life 6
   Early life.. 6
   Marriage and family life 9
   Other relationships 16
Public life before the White House 21
First Lady of the United States (1933–1945) 25
   American Youth Congress and National Youth Administration.. 27
   Arthurdale... 28
   Civil rights activism 30
   Norvelt.. 33
   Use of media.. 34
   World War II 38
Years after the White House 42
   United Nations.. 43
   Other postwar activities and honors 46
Death 51
Posthumous recognition 53
   Recognition and awards 53
   Places named for Roosevelt.. 55
Cultural references .... **Error! Bookmark not defined.**

Eleanor Roosevelt

Anna Eleanor Roosevelt (; October 11, 1884 – November 7, 1962) was an American political figure, diplomat and activist. She served as the First Lady of the United States from March 4, 1933, to April 12, 1945, during her husband President Franklin D. Roosevelt's four terms in office, making her the longest-serving First Lady of the United States. Roosevelt served as United States Delegate to the United Nations General Assembly from 1945 to 1952. President Harry S. Truman later called her the "First Lady of the World" in tribute to her human rights achievements.

Roosevelt was a member of the prominent American Roosevelt and Livingston families and a niece of President Theodore Roosevelt. She had an unhappy childhood, having suffered the deaths of both parents and one of her brothers at a young age. At 15, she attended Allenswood boarding Academy in London and was deeply influenced by its headmistress Marie Souvestre.

Returning to the U.S., she married her fifth cousin once removed, Franklin Delano Roosevelt, in 1905. The Roosevelts' marriage was complicated from the beginning by Franklin's controlling mother, Sara, and after Eleanor discovered her husband's affair with Lucy Mercer in 1918, she resolved to seek fulfillment in leading a public life of her own. She persuaded Franklin to stay in politics after he was stricken with a paralytic illness in 1921, which cost him the normal use of his legs, and began giving speeches and appearing at campaign events in his place. Following Franklin's election as Governor of New

York in 1928, and throughout the remainder of Franklin's public career in government, Roosevelt regularly made public appearances on his behalf; and as First Lady, while her husband served as president, she significantly reshaped and redefined the role of First Lady.

Though widely respected in her later years, Roosevelt was a controversial First Lady at the time for her outspokenness, particularly on civil rights for African-Americans. She was the first presidential spouse to hold regular press conferences, write a daily newspaper column, write a monthly magazine column, host a weekly radio show, and speak at a national party convention. On a few occasions, she publicly disagreed with her husband's policies.

She launched an experimental community at Arthurdale, West Virginia, for the families of unemployed miners, later widely regarded as a failure. She advocated for expanded roles for women in the workplace, the civil rights of African Americans and Asian Americans, and the rights of World War II refugees.

Following her husband's death in 1945, Roosevelt remained active in politics for the remaining 17 years of her life. She pressed the United States to join and support the United Nations and became its first delegate. She served as the first chair of the UN Commission on Human Rights and oversaw the drafting of the Universal Declaration of Human Rights.

Later, she chaired the John F. Kennedy administration's Presidential Commission on the Status of Women. By the time of her death, Roosevelt was regarded as "one of the most esteemed women in the world"; *The New York Times* called her "the object of almost universal respect" in an obituary.

In 1999, she was ranked ninth in the top ten of Gallup's List of Most Widely Admired People of the 20th Century.

Personal life

Early life

Anna Eleanor Roosevelt was born on October 11, 1884, in Manhattan, New York City, to socialites Anna Rebecca Hall and Elliott Bulloch Roosevelt. From an early age she preferred to be called by her middle name, Eleanor. Through her father, she was a niece of President Theodore Roosevelt. Through her mother, she was a niece of tennis champions Valentine Gill "Vallie" Hall III and Edward Ludlow Hall. Her mother nicknamed her "Granny" because she acted in such a serious manner as a child. Anna emotionally rejected Eleanor and was also somewhat ashamed of her daughter's alleged "plainness".

Roosevelt had two younger brothers: Elliott Jr. and Hall. She also had a half brother, Elliott Roosevelt Mann, through her father's affair with Katy Mann, a servant employed by the family. Roosevelt was born into a world of immense wealth and privilege, as her family was part of New York high society called the "swells".

On May 19, 1887, the two-year-old Roosevelt was onboard the *SS Britannic* with her father, mother and aunt Tissie, when it collided with White Star Liner *SS Celtic*. She was lowered into a lifeboat and she and her parents were taken to the *Celtic* and returned to New York. After this traumatic event, Eleanor was afraid of ships and the sea all her life.

Her mother died from diphtheria on December 7, 1892, and Elliott Jr. died of the same disease the following May.

Her father, an alcoholic confined to a sanitarium, died on August 14, 1894, after jumping from a window during a fit of delirium tremens. He survived the fall but died from a seizure. Roosevelt's childhood losses left her prone to depression throughout her life. Her brother Hall later suffered from alcoholism. Before her father died, he implored her to act as a mother towards Hall, and it was a request she made good upon for the rest of Hall's life.

Roosevelt doted on Hall, and when he enrolled at Groton School in 1907, she accompanied him as a chaperone. While he was attending Groton, she wrote him almost daily, but always felt a touch of guilt that Hall had not had a fuller childhood. She took pleasure in Hall's brilliant performance at school, and was proud of his many academic accomplishments, which included a master's degree in engineering from Harvard.

After the deaths of her parents, Roosevelt was raised in the household of her maternal grandmother, Mary Livingston Ludlow of the Livingston family in Tivoli, New York. As a child, she was insecure and starved for affection, and considered herself the "ugly duckling". However, Roosevelt wrote at 14 that one's prospects in life were not totally dependent on physical beauty: "no matter how plain a woman may be if truth and loyalty are stamped upon her face all will be attracted to her."

"If life were predictable it would cease to be life, and be without flavor."— Eleanor Roosevelt

Roosevelt was tutored privately and with the encouragement of her aunt Anna "Bamie" Roosevelt, she was sent to Allenswood Academy at the age of 15, a private finishing school in Wimbledon, outside London, England, where she was educated from 1899 to 1902. The headmistress, Marie Souvestre, was a noted educator who sought to cultivate independent thinking in young women. Souvestre took a special interest in Roosevelt, who learned to speak French fluently and gained self-confidence. Roosevelt and Souvestre maintained a correspondence until March 1905, when Souvestre died, and after this Roosevelt placed Souvestre's portrait on her desk and brought her letters with her.

Roosevelt's first cousin Corinne Douglas Robinson, whose first term at Allenswood overlapped with Roosevelt's last, said that when she arrived at the school, Roosevelt was " 'everything' at the school. She was beloved by everybody." Roosevelt wished to continue at Allenswood, but she was summoned home by her grandmother in 1902 to make her social debut.

At age 17 in 1902, Roosevelt completed her formal education and returned to the United States; she was presented at a debutante ball at the Waldorf-Astoria hotel on December 14. She was later given her own "coming out party". She said of her debut in a public discussion once, "It was simply awful. It was a beautiful party, of course, but I was so unhappy, because a girl who comes out is so utterly miserable if she does not know all the young people. Of course I had been so long abroad that I had lost touch with all the girls I used to know in New York. I was miserable through all that."

Roosevelt was active with the New York Junior League shortly after its founding, teaching dancing and calisthenics in the East Side slums. The organization had been brought to Roosevelt's attention by her friend, organization founder Mary Harriman, and a male relative who criticized the group for "drawing young women into public activity".

Roosevelt was a lifelong Episcopalian, regularly attended services, and was very familiar with the New Testament. Dr. Harold Ivan Smith states that she, "was very public about her faith. In hundreds of "My Day" and "If You Ask Me" columns, she addressed issues of faith, prayer and the Bible."

Fact: Eleanor earned 35 honorary degrees; FDR, meanwhile, only received 31 Among the institutions which bestowed degrees upon the First Lady-turned diplomat were Russell Sage College, the John Marshall College of Law, and Oxford University.

Marriage and family life

In the summer of 1902, Roosevelt encountered her father's fifth cousin, Franklin Delano Roosevelt, on a train to Tivoli, New York. The two began a secret correspondence and romance, and became engaged on November 22, 1903. Franklin's mother, Sara Ann Delano, opposed the union and made him promise that the engagement would not be officially announced for a year. "I know what pain I must have caused you," he wrote to his mother of his decision. But, he added, "I know my own mind, and known it for a long time, and know that I could never think otherwise." Sara took her son on a Caribbean cruise in 1904, hoping that a separation would squelch the romance, but Franklin remained determined.

The wedding date was set to accommodate President Theodore Roosevelt, who was scheduled to be in New York City for the St. Patrick's Day parade, and who agreed to give the bride away.

The couple were married on March 17, 1905, in a wedding officiated by Endicott Peabody, the groom's headmaster at Groton School. Her cousin Corinne Douglas Robinson was a bridesmaid. The marriage took place at Algonac, a family estate from Franklin's mother's family located in Newburgh. Theodore Roosevelt's attendance at the ceremony was front-page news in *The New York Times* and other newspapers. When asked for his thoughts on the Roosevelt–Roosevelt union, the president said, "It is a good thing to keep the name in the family." The couple spent a preliminary honeymoon of one week at Hyde Park, then set up housekeeping in an apartment in New York. That summer they went on their formal honeymoon, a three-month tour of Europe.

Fact: On her wedding day, then-president Teddy Roosevelt walked Eleanor down the aisle.

Returning to the U.S., the newlyweds settled in a New York City house that was provided by Franklin's mother, as well as in a second residence at the family's estate overlooking the Hudson River in Hyde Park, New York. From the beginning, Roosevelt had a contentious relationship with her controlling mother-in-law. The townhouse that Sara gave to them was connected to her own residence by sliding doors, and Sara ran both households in the decade after the marriage. Early on, Roosevelt had a breakdown in which she explained to Franklin that "I did not like to live in a house which was not in any way mine, one that I had done nothing about and which did not represent the way I wanted to live", but little changed. Sara also sought to control the raising of her grandchildren, and Roosevelt reflected later that "Franklin's children were more my mother-in-law's children than they were mine". Roosevelt's eldest son James remembered Sara telling her grandchildren, "Your mother only bore you, I am more your mother than your mother is."

Roosevelt and Franklin had six children:

- Anna Eleanor Roosevelt (1906–1975)

- James Roosevelt II (1907–1991)

- Franklin Roosevelt (1909–1909)

- Elliott Roosevelt (1910–1990)

- Franklin Delano Roosevelt Jr. (1914–1988)

- John Aspinwall Roosevelt (1916–1981)

Roosevelt disliked having sex with her husband. She once told her daughter Anna that it was an "ordeal to be borne". She also considered herself ill-suited to motherhood, later writing, "It did not come naturally to me to understand little children or to enjoy them".

In September 1918, Roosevelt was unpacking one of Franklin's suitcases when she discovered a bundle of love letters to him from her social secretary, Lucy Mercer. He had been contemplating leaving his wife for Mercer. However, following pressure from his political advisor, Louis Howe, and from his mother, who threatened to disinherit Franklin if he followed through with a divorce, the couple remained married. Their union from that point on was more of a political partnership. Disillusioned, Roosevelt again became active in public life, and focused increasingly on her social work rather than her role as a wife.

In August 1921, the family was vacationing at Campobello Island, New Brunswick, Canada, when Franklin was diagnosed with a paralytic illness, at the time believed to be polio. During the illness, through her nursing care, Roosevelt probably saved Franklin from death. His legs remained permanently paralyzed. When the extent of his disability became clear, Roosevelt fought a protracted battle with her mother-in-law over his future, persuading him to stay in politics despite Sara's urgings that he retire and become a country gentleman. Franklin's attending physician, Dr. William Keen, commended Roosevelt's devotion to the stricken Franklin during the time of his travail. "You have been a rare wife and have borne your heavy burden most bravely," he said, proclaiming her "one of my heroines".

This proved a turning point in Roosevelt and Sara's long-running struggle, and as Eleanor's public role grew, she increasingly broke from Sara's control. Tensions between Sara and Roosevelt over her new political friends rose to the point that the family constructed a cottage at Val-Kill, in which Roosevelt and her guests lived when Franklin and the children were away from Hyde Park. Roosevelt herself named the place Val-Kill, loosely translated as "waterfall-stream" from the Dutch language common to the original European settlers of the area. Franklin encouraged his wife to develop this property as a place where she could implement some of her ideas for work with winter jobs for rural workers and women.

Each year, when Roosevelt held a picnic at Val-Kill for delinquent boys, her granddaughter Eleanor Roosevelt Seagraves assisted her. She was close to her grandmother throughout her life. Seagraves concentrated her career as an educator and librarian on keeping alive many of the causes Roosevelt began and supported.

"It is not more vacation we need — it is more vocation."
— Eleanor Roosevelt

In 1924, she campaigned for Democrat Alfred E. Smith in his successful re-election bid as governor of New York State against the Republican nominee, her first cousin Theodore Roosevelt Jr. Theodore Jr. never forgave her. Eleanor's aunt, Anna "Bamie" Roosevelt Cowles, publicly broke with her after the election. She wrote to her niece, "I just hate to have Eleanor let herself look as she does. Though never handsome, she always had to me a charming effect, but alas and lackaday! Since politics have become her choicest interest all her charm has disappeared..." Roosevelt dismissed Bamie's criticisms by referring to her as an "aged woman". However, Bamie and Roosevelt eventually reconciled.

Theodore's elder daughter Alice also broke with Roosevelt over her campaign. Alice and her aunt reconciled after the latter wrote Alice a comforting letter upon the death of Alice's daughter, Paulina Longworth.

Roosevelt and her daughter Anna became estranged after she took over some of her mother's social duties at the White House. The relationship was further strained because Roosevelt desperately wanted to go with her husband to Yalta in February 1945 (two months before FDR's death), but he took Anna instead. A few years later, the two were able to reconcile and cooperate on numerous projects. Anna took care of her mother when she was terminally ill in 1962.

Roosevelt's son Elliott authored numerous books, including a mystery series in which his mother was the detective. However, these murder mysteries were researched and written by William Harrington. They continued until Harrington's death in 2000, ten years after Elliott's death. With James Brough, Elliot also wrote a highly personal book about his parents called *The Roosevelts of Hyde Park: An Untold Story*, in which he revealed details about the sexual lives of his parents, including his father's relationships with mistress Lucy Mercer and secretary Marguerite ("Missy") LeHand, as well as graphic details surrounding the illness that crippled his father.

Published in 1973, the biography also contains valuable insights into FDR's run for vice president, his rise to the governorship of New York, and his capture of the presidency in 1932, particularly with the help of Louis Howe. When Elliott published this book in 1973, Franklin Delano Roosevelt Jr. led the family's denunciation of him; the book was fiercely repudiated by all Elliot's siblings. Another of the siblings, James, published *My Parents, a Differing View* (with Bill Libby, 1976), which was written in part as a response to Elliot's book. A sequel to *An Untold Story* with James Brough, published in 1975 and titled *A Rendezvous With Destiny*, carried the Roosevelt saga to the end of World War II. *Mother R.: Eleanor Roosevelt's Untold Story*, also with Brough, was published in 1977. *Eleanor Roosevelt, with Love: A Centenary Remembrance*, came out in 1984.

Other relationships

In the 1930s, Roosevelt had a very close relationship with legendary aviator Amelia Earhart (1897–1937). One time, the two snuck out from the White House and went to a party dressed up for the occasion. After flying with Earhart, Roosevelt obtained a student permit but did not further pursue her plans to learn to fly. Franklin was not in favor of his wife becoming a pilot. Nevertheless, the two women communicated frequently throughout their lives.

Roosevelt also had a close relationship with Associated Press (AP) reporter Lorena Hickok (1893–1968), who covered her during the last months of the presidential campaign and "fell madly in love with her". During this period, Roosevelt wrote daily 10- to 15-page letters to "Hick", who was planning to write a biography of the First Lady. The letters included such endearments as, "I want to put my arms around you & kiss you at the corner of your mouth," and, "I can't kiss you, so I kiss your 'picture' good night and good morning!"

At Franklin's 1933 inauguration, Roosevelt wore a sapphire ring Hickok had given her. FBI Director J. Edgar Hoover despised Roosevelt's liberalism, her stance regarding civil rights, and criticisms of Hoover's surveillance tactics by both her and her husband, and so Hoover maintained a large file on Roosevelt, which the filmmakers of the biopic *J. Edgar* (2011) indicate included compromising evidence of this relationship, which Hoover intended to blackmail Roosevelt with. Compromised as a reporter, Hickok soon resigned her position with the AP to be closer to Roosevelt, who secured her a job as an investigator for a New Deal program.

There is considerable debate about whether or not Roosevelt had a sexual relationship with Hickok. It was known in the White House press corps at the time that Hickok was a lesbian. Scholars, including Lillian Faderman and Hazel Rowley, have asserted that there was a physical component to the relationship, while Hickok biographer Doris Faber has argued that the insinuative phrases have misled historians.

Doris Kearns Goodwin stated in her 1994 Pulitzer Prize–winning account of the Roosevelts that "whether Hick and Eleanor went beyond kisses and hugs" could not be determined with certainty. Roosevelt was close friends with several lesbian couples, such as Nancy Cook and Marion Dickerman, and Esther Lape and Elizabeth Fisher Read, suggesting that she understood lesbianism; Marie Souvestre, Roosevelt's childhood teacher and a great influence on her later thinking, was also a lesbian. Faber published some of Roosevelt and Hickok's correspondence in 1980, but concluded that the lovestruck phrasing was simply an "unusually belated schoolgirl crush" and warned historians not to be misled. Researcher Leila J. Rupp criticized Faber's argument, calling her book "a case study in homophobia" and arguing that Faber unwittingly presented "page after page of evidence that delineates the growth and development of a love affair between the two women".

In 1992, Roosevelt biographer Blanche Wiesen Cook argued that the relationship was in fact romantic, generating national attention. A 2011 essay by Russell Baker reviewing two new Roosevelt biographies in the *New York Review of Books* (*Franklin and Eleanor: An Extraordinary Marriage*, by Hazel Rowley, and *Eleanor Roosevelt: Transformative First Lady*, by Maurine H. Beasley) stated, "That the Hickok relationship was indeed erotic now seems beyond dispute considering what is known about the letters they exchanged."

In the same years, Washington gossip linked Roosevelt romantically with New Deal administrator Harry Hopkins, with whom she worked closely. Roosevelt also had a close relationship with New York State Police sergeant Earl Miller, who was assigned by the president to be her bodyguard. Roosevelt was 44 years old when she met Miller, 32, in 1929. He became her friend as well as her official escort, teaching her different sports, such as diving and riding, and coached her in tennis. Biographer Blanche Wiesen Cook writes that Miller was Roosevelt's "first romantic involvement" in her middle years. Hazel Rowley concludes, "There is no doubt that Eleanor was in love with Earl for a time ... But they are most unlikely to have had an 'affair'."

Roosevelt's friendship with Miller occurred at the same time that her husband had a rumored relationship with his secretary, Marguerite "Missy" LeHand. Smith writes, "remarkably, both ER and Franklin recognized, accepted, and encouraged the arrangement... Eleanor and Franklin were strong-willed people who cared greatly for each other's happiness but realized their own inability to provide for it." Roosevelt and Miller's relationship is said to have continued until her death in 1962. They are thought to have corresponded daily, but all letters have been lost. According to rumor, the letters were anonymously purchased and destroyed, or locked away when she died.

Roosevelt was a longtime friend of Carrie Chapman Catt and gave her the Chi Omega award at the White House in 1941.

Anti-Semitism

Eleanor Roosevelt in private showed a revulsion against rich Jews in 1918, telling her mother-in-law the "Jew party [was] appalling.... I never wish to hear money, jewels or sables mentioned again.". When she became co-owner of the Todhunter school in New York City, a limited number of Jews were admitted. Most students were upper-class Protestants, and Roosevelt said that the spirit of the school "would be different if we had too large a proportion of Jewish children." She said the problem is not just quantity but quality, since Jews were "very unlike ourselves" and had not yet become American enough. Her anti-Semitism gradually declined, especially as her friendship with Bernard Baruch grew. After World War II she became a staunch champion of Israel, which she admired for its commitment to New Deal values.

"There is no doubt that there is a need for improving the understanding and co-operation between the various races which make up the U.S.A., and perhaps the best place to begin is with the Jews and colored people." — Eleanor Roosevelt

Public life before the White House

In the 1920 presidential election, Franklin was nominated as the running mate of Democratic presidential candidate James M. Cox. Roosevelt joined Franklin in touring the country, making her first campaign appearances. Cox was defeated by Republican Warren G. Harding, who won with 404 electoral votes to 127.

Following the onset of Franklin's paralytic illness in 1921, Roosevelt began serving as a stand-in for her incapacitated husband, making public appearances on his behalf, often carefully coached by Louis Howe. She also started working with the Women's Trade Union League (WTUL), raising funds in support of the union's goals: a 48-hour workweek, minimum wage, and the abolition of child labor.

Throughout the 1920s, Roosevelt became increasingly influential as a leader in the New York State Democratic Party while Franklin used her contacts among Democratic women to strengthen his standing with them, winning their committed support for the future.

In 1924, she campaigned for Democrat Alfred E. Smith in his successful re-election bid as governor of New York State against the Republican nominee and her first cousin Theodore Roosevelt Jr. Franklin had spoken out on Theodore's "wretched record" as Assistant Secretary of the Navy during the Teapot Dome scandal, and in return, Theodore said of him, "He's a maverick! He does not wear the brand of our family," which infuriated her. She dogged Theodore on the New York State campaign trail in a car fitted with a *papier-mâché* bonnet shaped like a giant teapot that was made to emit simulated steam (to remind voters of Theodore's supposed, but later disproved, connections to the scandal), and countered his speeches with those of her own, calling him immature. She would later decry these methods, admitting that they were below her dignity but saying that they had been contrived by Democratic Party "dirty tricksters."

Theodore was defeated by 105,000 votes, and he never forgave her. By 1928, Roosevelt was promoting Smith's candidacy for president and Franklin's nomination as the Democratic Party's candidate for governor of New York, succeeding Smith. Although Smith lost the presidential race, Franklin won and the Roosevelts moved into the governor's mansion in Albany, New York. During Franklin's term as governor, Roosevelt traveled widely in the state to make speeches and inspect state facilities on his behalf, reporting her findings to him at the end of each trip.

In 1927, she joined friends Marion Dickerman and Nancy Cook in buying the Todhunter School for Girls, a finishing school which also offered college preparatory courses, in New York City. At the school, Roosevelt taught upper-level courses in American literature and history, emphasizing independent thought, current events, and social engagement. She continued to teach three days a week while FDR served as governor, but was forced to leave teaching after his election as president.

Also in 1927, she established Val-Kill Industries with Cook, Dickerman, and Caroline O'Day, three friends she met through her activities in the Women's Division of the

New York State Democratic Party. It was located on the banks of a stream that flowed through the Roosevelt family estate in Hyde Park, New York. Roosevelt and her business partners financed the construction of a small factory to provide supplemental income for local farming families who would make furniture, pewter, and homespun cloth using traditional craft methods. Capitalizing on the popularity of the Colonial Revival, most Val-Kill products were modeled on eighteenth-century forms.

Roosevelt promoted Val-Kill through interviews and public appearances. Val-Kill Industries never became the subsistence program that Roosevelt and her friends imagined, but it did pave the way for larger New Deal initiatives during Franklin's presidential administration. Cook's failing health and pressures from the Great Depression compelled the women to dissolve the partnership in 1938, at which time Roosevelt converted the shop buildings into a cottage at Val-Kill, that eventually became her permanent residence after Franklin died in 1945. Otto Berge acquired the contents of the factory and the use of the Val-Kill name to continue making colonial-style furniture until he retired in 1975.

In 1977, Roosevelt's cottage at Val-Kill and its surrounding property of 181 acres (0.73 km2), was formally designated by an act of Congress as the Eleanor Roosevelt National Historic Site, "to commemorate for the education, inspiration, and benefit of present and future generations the life and work of an outstanding woman in American history."

First Lady of the United States (1933–1945)

Roosevelt became First Lady of the United States when Franklin was inaugurated on March 4, 1933. Having known all of the twentieth century's previous First Ladies, she was seriously depressed at having to assume the role, which had traditionally been restricted to domesticity and hostessing. Her immediate predecessor, Lou Henry Hoover, had ended her feminist activism on becoming First Lady, stating her intention to be only a "backdrop for Bertie." Eleanor's distress at these precedents was severe enough that Hickok subtitled her biography of Roosevelt "Reluctant First Lady".

With support from Howe and Hickok, Roosevelt set out to redefine the position. According to her biographer Blanche Wiesen Cook, she became "the most controversial First Lady in United States history" in the process. Despite criticism of them both, with her husband's strong support she continued with the active business and speaking agenda she had begun before assuming the role of First Lady in an era when few married women had careers. She was the first presidential spouse to hold regular press conferences and in 1940 became the first to speak at a national party convention. She also wrote a daily and widely syndicated newspaper column, "My Day", another first for a presidential spouse. She was also the first First Lady to write a monthly magazine column and to host a weekly radio show.

In the first year of her husband's administration, Roosevelt was determined to match his presidential salary, and she earned $75,000 from her lectures and writing, most of which she gave to charity. By 1941, she was receiving lecture fees of $1,000, and was made an honorary member of Phi Beta Kappa at one of her lectures to celebrate her achievements.

Roosevelt maintained a heavy travel schedule in her twelve years in the White House, frequently making personal appearances at labor meetings to assure Depression-era workers that the White House was mindful of their plight. In one famous cartoon of the time from *The New Yorker* magazine (June 3, 1933), satirizing a visit she had made to a mine, an astonished coal miner, peering down a dark tunnel, says to a co-worker, "For gosh sakes, here comes Mrs. Roosevelt!"

In early 1933, the "Bonus Army", a protest group of World War I veterans, marched on Washington for the second time in two years, calling for their veteran bonus certificates to be awarded early. The previous year, President Hoover had ordered them dispersed, and the US Army cavalry charged and bombarded the veterans with tear gas. This time, Roosevelt visited the veterans at their muddy campsite, listening to their concerns and singing army songs with them. The meeting defused the tension between the veterans and the administration, and one of the marchers later commented, "Hoover sent the Army. [President] Roosevelt sent his wife."

In 1933 after she became First Lady, a new hybrid tea rose was named after her (Rosa x hybrida "Mrs. Franklin D. Roosevelt").

In 1937 she began writing her autobiography, all volumes of which were compiled into *The Autobiography of Eleanor Roosevelt* in 1961 (Harper & Brothers, ISBN 0-306-80476-X).

"The future belongs to those who believe in the beauty of their dreams." — Eleanor Roosevelt

American Youth Congress and National Youth Administration

The American Youth Congress (AYC) was formed in 1935 to advocate for youth rights in U.S. politics, and it was responsible for introducing the *American Youth Bill of Rights* to the U.S. Congress. Roosevelt's relationship with the AYC eventually led to the formation of the National Youth Administration, a New Deal agency in the United States, founded in 1935, that focused on providing work and education for Americans between the ages of 16 and 25. The NYA was headed by Aubrey Willis Williams, a prominent liberal from Alabama who was close to Roosevelt and Harry Hopkins. Speaking of the NYA in the 1930s, Roosevelt expressed her concern about ageism, stating that "I live in real terror when I think we may be losing this generation. We have got to bring these young people into the active life of the community and make them feel that they are necessary."

In 1939 the Dies Committee subpoenaed leaders of the AYC, who, in addition to serving the AYC, also were members of the Young Communist League. Roosevelt was in attendance at the hearings and afterward invited the subpoenaed witnesses to board at the White House during their stay in Washington D.C. Joseph P. Lash was one of her boarders. On February 10, 1940, members of the AYC, as guests of Roosevelt in her capacity as First Lady, attended a picnic on the White House lawn where they were addressed by Franklin from the South Portico. The President admonished them to condemn not merely the Nazi regime but all dictatorships. The President was reportedly booed by the group. Afterwards, many of the same youth picketed the White House as representatives of the American Peace Mobilization. Among them was Joseph Cadden, one of Roosevelt's overnight boarders. Later in 1940, despite Roosevelt's publication of her reasons "Why I still believe in the Youth Congress," the American Youth Congress was disbanded. The NYA was shut down in 1943.

Arthurdale

Roosevelt's chief project during her husband's first two terms was the establishment of a planned community in Arthurdale, West Virginia. On August 18, 1933, at Hickok's urging, Roosevelt visited the families of homeless miners in Morgantown, West Virginia, who had been blacklisted following union activities. Deeply affected by the visit, Roosevelt proposed a resettlement community for the miners at Arthurdale, where they could make a living by subsistence farming, handicrafts, and a local manufacturing plant. She hoped the project could become a model for "a new kind of community" in the U.S., in which workers would be better cared for. Her husband enthusiastically supported the project.

After an initial, disastrous experiment with prefab houses, construction began again in 1934 to Roosevelt's specifications, this time with "every modern convenience", including indoor plumbing and central steam heat. Families occupied the first fifty homes in June, and agreed to repay the government in thirty years' time. Though Roosevelt had hoped for a racially mixed community, the miners insisted on limiting membership to white Christians. After losing a community vote, Roosevelt recommended the creation of other communities for the excluded black and Jewish miners. The experience motivated Roosevelt to become much more outspoken on the issue of racial discrimination.

Roosevelt remained a vigorous fundraiser for the community for several years, as well as spending most of her own income on the project. However, the project was criticized by both the political left and right. Conservatives condemned it as socialist and a "communist plot", while Democratic members of Congress opposed government competition with private enterprise. Secretary of the Interior Harold Ickes also opposed the project, citing its high per-family cost. Arthurdale continued to sink as a government spending priority for the federal government until 1941, when the U.S. sold off the last of its holdings in the community at a loss.

Later commentators generally described the Arthurdale experiment as a failure. Roosevelt herself was sharply discouraged by a 1940 visit in which she felt the town had become excessively dependent on outside assistance. However, the residents considered the town a "utopia" compared to their previous circumstances, and many were returned to economic self-sufficiency. Roosevelt personally considered the project a success, later speaking of the improvements she saw in people's lives there and stating, "I don't know whether you think that is worth half a million dollars. But I do."

Civil rights activism

During Franklin's administration, Roosevelt became an important connection to the African-American population in the era of segregation. Despite the President's desire to placate Southern sentiment, Roosevelt was vocal in her support of the civil rights movement. After her experience with Arthurdale and her inspections of New Deal programs in Southern states, she concluded that New Deal programs were discriminating against African-Americans, who received a disproportionately small share of relief money. Roosevelt became one of the only voices in her husband's administration insisting that benefits be equally extended to Americans of all races.

Roosevelt also broke with tradition by inviting hundreds of African-American guests to the White House. In 1936 she became aware of conditions at the National Training School for Girls, a predominantly black reform school once located in the Palisades neighborhood of Washington, D.C. She visited the school, wrote about it in her "My Day" column, lobbied for additional funding, and pressed for changes in staffing and curriculum. Her White House invitation to the students became an issue in Franklin's 1936 re-election campaign.

When the black singer Marian Anderson was denied the use of Washington's Constitution Hall by the Daughters of the American Revolution in 1939, Roosevelt resigned from the group in protest and helped arrange another concert on the steps of the Lincoln Memorial. Roosevelt later presented Anderson to the King and Queen of the United Kingdom after Anderson performed at a White House dinner. Roosevelt also arranged the appointment of African-American educator Mary McLeod Bethune, with whom she had struck up a friendship, as Director of the Division of Negro Affairs of the National Youth Administration. To avoid problems with the staff when Bethune would visit the White House, Roosevelt would meet her at the gate, embrace her, and walk in with her arm-in-arm.

She was involved by being "the eyes and the ears" of the New Deal. She looked to the future and was committed to social reform. One of those programs helped working women receive better wages. The New Deal also placed women into less machine work and more white-collar work. Women did not have to work in the factories making war supplies because men were coming home so they could take over the long days and nights women had been working to contribute to the war efforts. Roosevelt brought unprecedented activism and ability to the role of the First Lady.

In contrast to her usual support of African-American rights, the "sundown town" Eleanor, in West Virginia, was named for her and was established in 1934 when she and Franklin visited the county and developed it as a test site for families. As a "sundown town", like other Franklin Roosevelt towns around the nation (such as Greenbelt, Greenhills, Greendale, Hanford, or Norris), it was for whites only. It was established as a New Deal project.

Roosevelt lobbied behind the scenes for the 1934 Costigan-Wagner Bill to make lynching a federal crime, including arranging a meeting between Franklin and NAACP president Walter Francis White. Fearing he would lose the votes of Southern congressional delegations for his legislative agenda, however, Franklin refused to publicly support the bill, which proved unable to pass the Senate.

In 1942, Roosevelt worked with activist Pauli Murray to persuade Franklin to appeal on behalf of sharecropper Odell Waller, convicted of killing a white farmer during a fight; though Franklin sent a letter to Virginia Governor Colgate Darden urging him to commute the sentence to life imprisonment, Waller was executed as scheduled.

Roosevelt's support of African-American rights made her an unpopular figure among whites in the South. Rumors spread of "Eleanor Clubs" formed by servants to oppose their employers and "Eleanor Tuesdays" on which

African-American men would knock down white women on the street, though no evidence has ever been found of either practice. When race riots broke out in Detroit in June 1943, critics in both the North and South wrote that Roosevelt was to blame. At the same time, she grew so popular among African-Americans, previously a reliable Republican voting bloc, that they became a consistent base of support for the Democratic Party.

Following the Japanese attack on Pearl Harbor on December 7, 1941, Roosevelt spoke out against Japanese-American prejudice, warning against the "great hysteria against minority groups." She also privately opposed her husband's Executive Order 9066, which required Japanese-Americans in many areas of the U.S. to enter internment camps. She was widely criticized for her defense of Japanese-American citizens, including a call by the *Los Angeles Times* that she be "forced to retire from public life" over her stand on the issue.

Norvelt

"We are afraid to care too much, for fear that the other person does not care at all." — Eleanor Roosevelt

On May 21, 1937, Roosevelt visited Westmoreland Homesteads to mark the arrival of the community's final homesteader. Accompanying her on the trip was the wife of Henry Morgenthau Jr., the president's Secretary of the Treasury. "I am no believer in paternalism. I do not like charities," she had said earlier. But cooperative communities such as Westmoreland Homesteads, she went on, offered an alternative to "our rather settled ideas" that could "provide equality of opportunity for all and prevent the recurrence of a similar disaster [depression] in the future." Residents were so taken by her personal expression of interest in the program that they promptly agreed to rename the community in her honor. (The new town name, Norvelt, was a combination of the last syllables in her names: EleaNOR RooseVELT.) The Norvelt firefighter's hall is named Roosevelt Hall in honor of her.

Use of media

Roosevelt was an unprecedentedly outspoken First Lady who made far more use of the media than her predecessors; she held 348 press conferences over the span of her husband's 12-year presidency. Inspired by her relationship with Hickok, Roosevelt placed a ban on male reporters attending the press conferences, effectively forcing newspapers to keep female reporters on staff in order to cover them. She relaxed the rule only once, on her return from her 1943 Pacific trip. Because the Gridiron Club banned women from its annual Gridiron Dinner for journalists, Roosevelt hosted a competing event for female reporters at the White House, which she called "Gridiron Widows". She was interviewed by many newspapers; the New Orleans journalist Iris Kelso described Roosevelt as her most interesting interviewee ever.

In the early days of her all-female press conferences, she said they would not address "politics, legislation, or executive decision", since the role of the First Lady was expected to be non-political at that time. She also agreed at first that she would avoid discussing her views on pending congressional measures. Still, the press conferences provided a welcome opportunity for the women reporters to speak directly with the First Lady, access that had been unavailable in previous administrations.

Just before Franklin assumed the presidency in February 1933, Roosevelt published an editorial in the *Women's Daily News* that conflicted so sharply with his intended public spending policies that he published a rejoinder in the following issue. On entering the White House, she signed a contract with the magazine *Woman's Home Companion* to provide a monthly column, in which she answered mail sent to her by readers; the feature was canceled in 1936 as another presidential election approached. She continued her articles in other venues, publishing more than sixty articles in national magazines during her tenure as First Lady.

Roosevelt also began a syndicated newspaper column, titled "My Day", which appeared six days a week from 1936 to her death in 1962. In the column, she wrote about her daily activities but also her humanitarian concerns. Hickok and George T. Bye, Roosevelt's literary agent, encouraged her to write the column. From 1941 to her death in 1962, she also wrote an advice column, *If You Ask Me*, first published in *Ladies Home Journal* and then later in *McCall's*. A selection of her columns was compiled in the book *If You Ask Me: Essential Advice from Eleanor Roosevelt* in 2018.

Beasley has argued that Roosevelt's publications, which often dealt with women's issues and invited reader responses, represented a conscious attempt to use journalism "to overcome social isolation" for women by making "public communication a two-way channel".

Roosevelt also made extensive use of radio. She was not the first First Lady to broadcast—her predecessor, Lou Henry Hoover, had done that already. But Hoover did not have a regular radio program, whereas Roosevelt did. She first broadcast her own programs of radio commentary beginning on July 9, 1934. On that first show, she talked about the effect of movies on children, the need for a censor who could make sure movies did not glorify crime and violence, and her opinion about the recent All-Star baseball game. She also read a commercial from a mattress company, which sponsored the broadcast. She said she would not accept any salary for being on the air, and that she would donate the amount ($3,000) to charity.

Later that year, in November 1934, she broadcast a series of programs about children's education; it was heard on the CBS Radio Network. Sponsored by a typewriter company, Roosevelt once again donated the money, giving it to the American Friends Service Committee, to help with a school it operated. During 1934, Roosevelt set a record for the most times a First Lady had spoken on radio: she spoke as a guest on other people's programs, as well as the host of her own, for a total of 28 times that year.

In 1935, Roosevelt continued to host programs aimed at the female audience, including one called "It's A Woman's World." Each time, she donated the money she earned to charity. The association of a sponsor with the popular First Lady resulted in increases in sales for that company: when the Selby Shoe Company sponsored a series of Roosevelt's programs, sales increased by 200%. The fact that her programs were sponsored created controversy, with her husband's political enemies expressing skepticism about whether she really did donate her salary to charity; they accused her of "profiteering." But her radio programs proved to be so popular with listeners that the criticisms had little effect. She continued to broadcast throughout the 1930s, sometimes on CBS and sometimes on NBC.

Fact: Eleanor organized several women-only white house press conferences; At the time FDR was first elected president, female journalists had traditionally been excluded from serious media events at 1600 Pennsylvania Avenue. Eleanor helped to somewhat level the playing field by hosting a series of ladies-only press conferences, which pressured papers into hiring more women reporters and helped Eleanor win over female voters on behalf of her husband.

World War II

"I can not believe that war is the best solution. No one won the last war, and no one will win the next war."
— Eleanor Roosevelt

On May 10, 1940, Germany invaded Belgium, Luxembourg, and the Netherlands, marking the end of the relatively conflict-free "Phoney War" phase of World War II. As the U.S. began to move toward war footing, Roosevelt found herself again depressed, fearing that her role in fighting for domestic justice would become extraneous in a nation focused on foreign affairs. She briefly considered traveling to Europe to work with the Red Cross, but was dissuaded by presidential advisers who pointed out the consequences should the president's wife be captured as a prisoner of war.

She soon found other wartime causes to work on, however, beginning with a popular movement to allow the immigration of European refugee children. She also lobbied her husband to allow greater immigration of groups persecuted by the Nazis, including Jews, but fears of fifth columnists caused Franklin to restrict immigration rather than expanding it. Roosevelt successfully secured political refugee status for eighty-three Jewish refugees from the S.S. *Quanza* in August 1940, but was refused on many other occasions. Her son James later wrote that "her deepest regret at the end of her life" was that she had not forced Franklin to accept more refugees from Nazism during the war.

Roosevelt was also active on the home front. Beginning in 1941, she co-chaired the Office of Civilian Defense (OCD) with New York City Mayor Fiorello H. LaGuardia, working to give civilian volunteers expanded roles in war preparations. She soon found herself in a power struggle with LaGuardia, who preferred to focus on narrower aspects of defense, while she saw solutions to broader social problems as equally important to the war effort. Though LaGuardia resigned from the OCD in December 1941, Roosevelt was forced to resign following anger in the House of Representatives over high salaries for several OCD appointments, including two of her close friends.

Also in 1941, the short film *Women in Defense*, written by Roosevelt, was released. It was produced by the Office of Emergency Management and briefly outlines the way in which women could help prepare the country for the possibility of war. There is also a segment on the types of costumes women would wear while engaged in war work. At the end of the film, the narrator explains women are vital to securing a healthy American home life and raising children "which has always been the first line of defense".

In October 1942, Roosevelt toured England, visiting with American troops and inspecting British forces. Her visits drew enormous crowds and received almost unanimously favorable press in both England and America.

In August 1943, she visited American troops in the South Pacific on a morale-building tour, of which Admiral William Halsey Jr. later said, "she alone accomplished more good than any other person, or any groups of civilians, who had passed through my area." For her part,

Roosevelt was left shaken and deeply depressed by seeing the war's carnage. A number of Congressional Republicans criticized her for using scarce wartime resources for her trip, prompting Franklin to suggest that she take a break from traveling.

Roosevelt supported increased roles for women and African-Americans in the war effort, and began to advocate for women to be given factory jobs a year before it became a widespread practice.

In 1942, she urged women of all social backgrounds to learn trades, saying: "if I were of a debutante age I would go into a factory–any factory where I could learn a skill and be useful." Roosevelt learned of the high rate of absenteeism among working mothers, and she campaigned for government-sponsored day care. She notably supported the Tuskegee Airmen in their successful effort to become the first black combat pilots, visiting the Tuskegee Air Corps Advanced Flying School in Alabama. She also flew with African-American chief civilian instructor C. Alfred "Chief" Anderson. Anderson had been flying since 1929 and was responsible for training thousands of rookie pilots; he took her on a half-hour flight in a Piper J-3 Cub. After landing, she cheerfully announced, "Well, you can fly all right." The subsequent brouhaha over the First Lady's flight had such an impact it is often mistakenly cited as the start of the Civilian Pilot Training Program at Tuskegee, even though the program was already five months old. Roosevelt did use her position as a trustee of the Julius Rosenwald Fund to arrange a loan of $175,000 to help finance the building of Moton Field.

After the war, Roosevelt was a strong proponent of the Morgenthau Plan to de-industrialize Germany in the postwar period. In 1947 she attended the National Conference on the German Problem in New York, which she had helped organize. It issued a statement that "any plans to resurrect the economic and political power of Germany" would be dangerous to international security.

Years after the White House

Franklin died on April 12, 1945, after suffering a cerebral hemorrhage at the Little White House in Warm Springs, Georgia. Roosevelt later learned that her husband's mistress Lucy Mercer (now named Rutherfurd) had been with him when he died, a discovery made more bitter by learning that her daughter Anna had also been aware of the ongoing relationship between the President and Rutherfurd. It was Anna who told her that Franklin had been with Rutherfurd when he died; in addition, she told her that Franklin had continued the relationship for decades, and people surrounding him had hidden the information from his wife. After the funeral, Roosevelt temporarily returned to Val-Kill. Franklin left instructions for her in the event of his death; he proposed turning over Hyde Park to the federal government as a museum, and she spent the following months cataloging the estate and arranging for the transfer.

After Franklin's death, she moved into an apartment at 29 Washington Square West in Greenwich Village. In 1950, she rented suites at the Park Sheraton Hotel (202 West 56th Street). She lived here until 1953 when she moved to 211 East 62nd Street. When that lease expired in 1958, she returned to the Park Sheraton as she waited for the house she purchased with Edna and David Gurewitsch at 55 East 74th Street to be renovated. The Franklin D. Roosevelt Presidential Library and Museum opened on April 12, 1946, setting a precedent for future presidential libraries.

United Nations

In December 1945, President Harry S. Truman appointed Roosevelt as a delegate to the United Nations General Assembly. In April 1946, she became the first chairperson of the preliminary United Nations Commission on Human Rights. Roosevelt remained chairperson when the commission was established on a permanent basis in January 1947. Along with René Cassin, John Peters Humphrey and others, she played an instrumental role in drafting the Universal Declaration of Human Rights (UDHR).

In a speech on the night of September 28, 1948, Roosevelt spoke in favor of the Declaration, calling it "the international Magna Carta of all men everywhere". The

Declaration was adopted by the General Assembly on December 10, 1948. The vote was unanimous, with eight abstentions: six Soviet Bloc countries as well as South Africa and Saudi Arabia. Roosevelt attributed the abstention of the Soviet bloc nations to Article 13, which provided the right of citizens to leave their countries.

The following is a fragment of that speech:

"We must not be confused about what freedom is. Basic human rights are simple and easily understood: freedom of speech and a free press; freedom of religion and worship; freedom of assembly and the right of petition; the right of men to be secure in their homes and free from unreasonable search and seizure and from arbitrary arrest and punishment.

We must not be deluded by the efforts of the forces of reaction to prostitute the great words of our free tradition and thereby to confuse the struggle. Democracy, freedom, human rights have come to have a definite meaning to the people of the world which we must not allow any nation to so change that they are made synonymous with suppression and dictatorship.

There are basic differences that show up even in the use of words between a democratic and a totalitarian country. For instance "democracy" means one thing to the U.S.S.R. and another the U.S.A. and, I know, in France. I have served since the first meeting of the nuclear commission on the Human Rights Commission, and I think this point stands out clearly."

Roosevelt also served as the first United States Representative to the United Nations Commission on Human Rights and stayed on at that position until 1953, even after stepping down as chair of the commission in 1951. The UN posthumously awarded her one of its first Human Rights Prizes in 1968 in recognition of her work.

In the 1940s, Roosevelt was among the first people to support the creation of a UN agency specialized in the issues of food and nutrition.

At that time, Frederick L. McDougall, an Australian nutritionist, wrote the "Draft memorandum on a United Nations Programme for Freedom from Want of Food". McDougall strongly believed that international cooperation was key to address the issue of hunger in the world.

Roosevelt learned about the memorandum and arranged a meeting between McDougall and her husband, the president of the United States of America. Following the discussion, the Food and Agriculture Organization of the United Nations (FAO) was created on 16 October 1945.

In 1955, Eleanor Roosevelt and McDougall visited the new FAO headquarters in Rome and pushed the United Nations Programme into creating the Food from Hunger campaign, which ultimately saw the light in 1960 after a series of negotiations.

The Campaign was created to mobilize non-governmental organizations against hunger and malnutrition in the world and help find solutions.

Other postwar activities and honors

"The world of the future is in our making. Tomorrow is now." — Eleanor Roosevelt

In the late 1940s, Democrats in New York and throughout the country courted Roosevelt for political office.

Catholics comprised a major element of the Democratic Party in New York City. Roosevelt supported reformers trying to overthrow the Irish machine Tammany Hall, and some Catholics called her anti-Catholic. In July 1949, Roosevelt had a bitter public disagreement with Cardinal Francis Spellman, the Archbishop of New York, over federal funding for parochial schools. Spellman said she was anti-Catholic, and supporters of both took sides in a battle that drew national attention and is "still remembered for its vehemence and hostility."

In 1949, she was made an honorary member of the historically black organization Alpha Kappa Alpha.

She was an early supporter of the Encampment for Citizenship, a non-profit organization that conducts residential summer programs with year-round follow-up for young people of widely diverse backgrounds and nations. She routinely hosted encampment workshops at her Hyde Park estate, and when the program was attacked as "socialistic" by McCarthyite forces in the early 1950s, she vigorously defended it.

Eleanor Roosevelt's Speech on Human Rights

On December 10, 1951, gave a speech in the third anniversary of the declaration of human rights from St.Louis, Missouri.

The following is a fragment of that speech:

"I'm very glad to be able to take part in this celebration in St. Louis on Human Rights Day. Ever since the declaration of human rights, the Universal Declaration of Human Rights, was passed in Paris in 1948 on December the 10th, we have fostered the observance of this day not only in the United States but throughout the world.

The object is to make people everywhere conscious of the importance of human rights and freedoms.

The reason for that is that these are spoken of and emphasized in the Charter of the United Nations, and the declaration was written to elaborate the rights already mentioned in the charter and to emphasize also, for all of us, the fact that the building of human rights would be one of the foundation stones, on which we would build in the world, an atmosphere in which peace can grow.

For that reason, all over the world we've encouraged the Association for the United Nations to observe a whole week before United Nations Day comes around to explain the United Nations and what goes on in that organization and when we come to the celebration for human rights we try to particularly have people study the declaration so that they will really understand what were considered to be the most essential rights for all people to have throughout the world."

In 1954, Tammany Hall boss Carmine DeSapio led the effort to defeat Roosevelt's son, Franklin Delano Roosevelt Jr., in the election for New York Attorney General. Roosevelt grew increasingly disgusted with DeSapio's political conduct through the rest of the 1950s. Eventually, she would join with her old friends Herbert Lehman and Thomas Finletter to form the New York Committee for Democratic Voters, a group dedicated to opposing DeSapio's reincarnated Tammany Hall. Their efforts were eventually successful, and DeSapio was forced to relinquish power in 1961.

Roosevelt was disappointed when President Truman backed New York Governor W. Averell Harriman—a close associate of DeSapio—for the 1952 Democratic presidential nomination. She supported Adlai Stevenson for president in 1952 and 1956, and urged his renomination in 1960. She resigned from her UN post in 1953, when Dwight D. Eisenhower became president. She addressed the Democratic National Convention in 1952 and 1956. Although she had reservations about John F. Kennedy for his failure to condemn McCarthyism, she supported him for president against Richard Nixon. Kennedy later reappointed her to the United Nations, where she served again from 1961 to 1962, and to the National Advisory Committee of the Peace Corps.

By the 1950s, Roosevelt's international role as spokesperson for women led her to stop publicly criticizing the Equal Rights Amendment (ERA), although she never supported it. In the early 1960s, she announced that, due to unionization, she believed the ERA was no longer a threat to women as it once may have been and told supporters that they could have the amendment if they wanted it.

In 1961, President Kennedy's undersecretary of labor, Esther Peterson, proposed a new Presidential Commission on the Status of Women. Kennedy appointed Roosevelt to chair the commission, with Peterson as director. This was Roosevelt's last public position. She died just before the commission issued its report. It concluded that female equality was best achieved by recognition of gender differences and needs, and not by an Equal Rights Amendment.

Throughout the 1950s, Roosevelt embarked on countless national and international speaking engagements. She continued to pen her newspaper column and made appearances on television and radio broadcasts. She averaged one hundred fifty lectures a year throughout the 1950s, many devoted to her activism on behalf of the United Nations.

Roosevelt received the first annual Franklin Delano Roosevelt Brotherhood Award in 1946. Other notable awards she received during her life postwar included the Award of Merit of the New York City Federation of Women's Clubs in 1948, the Four Freedoms Award in 1950, the Irving Geist Foundation Award in 1950, and the Prince Carl Medal (from Sweden) in 1950. She was the most admired living woman, according to Gallup's most admired man and woman poll of Americans, every year between 1948 (the poll's inception) to 1961 (the last poll before her death) except 1951.

Following the Bay of Pigs in 1961, President Kennedy asked Roosevelt, labor leader Walter Reuther, and Milton S. Eisenhower, brother of President Eisenhower, to negotiate the release of captured Americans with Cuban leader Fidel Castro.

Death

In April 1960, Roosevelt was diagnosed with aplastic anemia soon after being struck by a car in New York City. In 1962, she was given steroids, which activated a dormant case of tuberculosis in her bone marrow, and she died of resulting cardiac failure at her Manhattan home at 55 East 74th Street on the Upper East Side on November 7, 1962, at the age of 78. Her daughter Anna took care of Roosevelt when she was terminally ill in 1962. President John F. Kennedy ordered all United States flags lowered to half-staff throughout the world on November 8 in tribute to Roosevelt.

Among other prominent attendees, President Kennedy, Vice President Lyndon Johnson and former presidents Truman and Eisenhower honored Roosevelt at funeral services in Hyde Park on November 10, 1962, where she was interred next to her husband in the Rose Garden at

"Springwood", the Roosevelt family home. At the services, Adlai Stevenson said: "What other single human being has touched and transformed the existence of so many?", adding, "She would rather light a candle than curse the darkness, and her glow has warmed the world."

After her death, her family deeded the family vacation home on Campobello Island to the governments of the U.S. and Canada, and in 1964 they created the 2,800-acre (11 km^2) Roosevelt Campobello International Park.

Posthumous recognition

Recognition and awards

In 1966, the White House Historical Association purchased Douglas Chandor's portrait of Eleanor Roosevelt; the portrait had been commissioned by the Roosevelt family in 1949. The painting was presented at a White House reception on February 4, 1966, that was hosted by Lady Bird Johnson and attended by more than 250 invited guests. The portrait hangs in the Vermeil Room.

Roosevelt was posthumously inducted into the National Women's Hall of Fame in 1973.

In 1989, the Eleanor Roosevelt Fund Award was founded; it "honors an individual, project, organization, or institution for outstanding contributions to equality and education for women and girls."

The Eleanor Roosevelt Monument in New York's Riverside Park was dedicated in 1996, with First Lady Hillary Clinton serving as the keynote speaker. It was the first monument to an American woman in a New York City park. The centerpiece is a statue of Roosevelt sculpted by Penelope Jencks. The surrounding granite pavement contains inscriptions designed by the architect Michael Middleton Dwyer, including summaries of her achievements, and a quote from her 1958 speech at the United Nations advocating universal human rights.

The following year, the Franklin Delano Roosevelt Memorial in Washington D.C. was dedicated; it includes a bronze statue of Eleanor Roosevelt standing before the United Nations emblem, which honors her dedication to the United Nations. It is the only presidential memorial to depict a First Lady.

"It isn't enough to talk about peace. One must believe in it. And it isn't enough to believe in it. One must work at it." — Eleanor Roosevelt

In 1998, President Bill Clinton established the Eleanor Roosevelt Award for Human Rights to honor outstanding American promoters of rights in the United States. The award was first awarded on the 50th anniversary of the Universal Declaration of Human Rights, honoring Eleanor Roosevelt's role as the "driving force" in the development of the UN's Universal Declaration of Human Rights. The award was presented from 1998 to the end of the Clinton Administration in 2001. In 2010, then-Secretary of State of the United States Hillary Clinton revived the Eleanor Roosevelt Award for Human Rights and presented the award on behalf of the then-President of the United States Barack Obama.

The Gallup Organization published the poll Gallup's List of Most Widely Admired People of the 20th Century, to determine which people around the world Americans most admired for what they did in the 20th century in 1999. Eleanor Roosevelt came in ninth. In 2001, the Eleanor Roosevelt Legacy Committee (Eleanor's Legacy) was founded by Judith Hollensworth Hope, who was its president until April 2008. It inspires and supports pro-choice Democratic women to run for local and state offices in New York. The Legacy sponsors campaign training schools, links candidates with volunteers and experts, collaborates with like-minded organizations and provides campaign grants to endorsed candidates. In 2007, she was named a Woman hero by The My Hero Project.

On April 20, 2016, United States Secretary of the Treasury Jacob Lew announced that Eleanor Roosevelt will appear with Marian Anderson and noted suffragettes on the redesigned US$5 bill scheduled to be unveiled in the year 2020, the 100th anniversary of the 19th Amendment of the U.S. Constitution, which guaranteed women the right to vote. In 2020, *Time* magazine included her name on its list of 100 Women of the Year. She was named Woman of the Year 1948 for her efforts on tackling issues surrounding human rights.

Places named for Roosevelt

In 1972, the Eleanor Roosevelt Institute was founded; it merged with the Franklin D. Roosevelt Four Freedoms Foundation in 1987 to become the Roosevelt Institute. The Roosevelt Institute is a liberal American think tank. The organization, based in New York City, states that it exists "to carry forward the legacy and values of Franklin and Eleanor Roosevelt by developing progressive ideas and bold leadership in the service of restoring America's promise of opportunity for all."

Eleanor Roosevelt High School, a public magnet high school specializing in science, mathematics, technology, and engineering, was established in 1976 at its current location in Greenbelt, Maryland. It was the first high school named for Eleanor Roosevelt, and is part of the Prince George's County Public Schools system.

Roosevelt lived in a stone cottage at Val-Kill, which was two miles east of the Springwood Estate. The cottage had been her home after the death of her husband and was the only residence she had ever personally owned. In 1977, the home was formally designated by an act of Congress as the Eleanor Roosevelt National Historic Site, "to commemorate for the education, inspiration, and benefit of present and future generations the life and work of an outstanding woman in American history."

In 1998, Save America's Treasures (SAT) announced Val-Kill cottage as a new official project. SAT's involvement led to the Honoring Eleanor Roosevelt (HER) project, initially run by private volunteers and now a part of SAT. The HER project has since raised almost $1 million, which has gone toward restoration and development efforts at Val-Kill and the production of *Eleanor Roosevelt: Close to Home*, a documentary about Roosevelt at Val-Kill. Due in part to the success of these programs, Val-Kill was given a $75,000 grant and named one of 12 sites showcased in *Restore America: A Salute to Preservation*, a partnership between SAT, the National Trust and HGTV.

The Roosevelt Study Center, a research institute, conference center, and library on twentieth-century American history located in the twelfth-century Abbey of Middelburg, the Netherlands, opened in 1986. It is named after Eleanor Roosevelt, Theodore Roosevelt, and Franklin Roosevelt, all of whose ancestors emigrated from Zeeland, the Netherlands, to the United States in the seventeenth century.

In 1988, Eleanor Roosevelt College, one of six undergraduate residential colleges at the University of California, San Diego, was founded. ERC emphasizes international understanding, including proficiency in a foreign language and a regional specialization. Eleanor Roosevelt High School, a small public high school on the Upper East Side of Manhattan in New York City, was founded in 2002. Eleanor Roosevelt High School in Eastvale, California, opened in 2006.